For Cotton ~
May you always know
how much God loves
you and your family! ♡

Joy and
Blessings, ☺
Saundra Sandrock

2016

Little Bits:

Spiritual Meditations for Little People

Little Bits:

Spiritual Meditations for Little People

SAUNDRA K. SANDROCK

Library of Congress Control Number:		2015919586
ISBN:	Hardcover	978-1-5144-2929-7
	Softcover	978-1-5144-2928-0
	eBook	978-1-5144-2927-3

New International Version (NIV)
Holy Bible, New International Version®, NIV® Copyright ©1973, 1978, 1984, 2011 byBiblica, Inc.® Used by permission. All rights reserved worldwide.

Any people depicted in stock imagery provided by Thinkstock are models, and such images are being used for illustrative purposes only.
Certain stock imagery © Thinkstock.

Print information available on the last page.

Rev. date: 11/24/2015

To order additional copies of this book, contact:
Xlibris
1-888-795-4274
www.Xlibris.com
Orders@Xlibris.com
730439

CONTENTS

Dedication

Dedicated to my adult children

Jennifer and Kevin

I am so blessed to be their mom!

~ Saundra K. Sandrock

About the Author

Saundra Sandrock was a classroom teacher in Pennsylvania for 25 years. She has a Master's Certification in Early Childhood Education. Her extensive Christian Education experiences include writing and presenting children's sermons, writing music and directing children's choirs, teaching Sunday School and Vacation Bible School.

Just One Me

When I look in the mirror,
A special face I see.
There is no other like it,
For God made just one me!

I know that when God made me,
He had a special plan.
And all God asks of me is
To be the best I can.

For each one's gifts are different.
God planned that too, I know.
So we can use our talents
To help each other grow.

I'm glad for who I am now,
And what I'm meant to be.
For I've a special place here
In God's big family!

"We are the work of God's hands."
Isaiah 64:8

Joyful Thoughts

What brings me joy
Besides a new toy?
I hope I can think of more.
God gave so much
To each little touch
I might not have noticed before.

Well there are birds
Who don't need words
To help me get awake.
And then there are clouds
Alone or in crowds.
Sky animals they seem to make.

I like to play
On a sunny day
And feel the warmth on my skin.
Outside is fun.
I like to run
While breathing the fresh air in.

When the sun's rays
Poke through cloudy haze
It looks like God has fingers.
After a storm,
God's paintbrush can form
An awesome rainbow that lingers.

Then there is snow.
In case you don't know,
No two flakes are the same.
And it's a treat
You just can't beat
To play a snowball game.

I'd fill a day
With so much to say
About the things I now feel.
These gifts of love from God above
Do bring me joy that's for real!

"It is good to give thanks to the Lord"
Psalm 92:1

God Never Runs Out of Ideas

God never runs out of ideas!
For that I am so glad.
If there was only one color,
That would be so very sad.

And what about the ocean
With so many shells to find?
It wouldn't be half the fun
If they were all the very same kind.

Only one type of flowers,
And just one type of trees?
It would be so confusing
To all the birds and bees!

Then if every person
Also looked the same...
How would we remember
Anybody's name?

So thanks to our Creator
For all that He has done,
To make the world we live in
A really interesting one!

"God saw all that he had made
and it was very good."

Genesis 1:31

Let Your Smile Shine

Let your smile shine.
It'll make you feel fine.
God's love is true.
He's always with you,
So let your smile shine!

You are blessed with a mind
Of the very best kind.
You have freedom to choose.
What a privilege to use
Your wonderful mind!

Just let your light shine.
It'll make you feel fine.
Just ask God in prayer.
He will always be there
To help your light shine!

"I will be glad and rejoice in God's love."

Psalm 31:7

Joyful Giver

If you really want to be happy,
Start now to joyfully give.
When you learn to think of others,
Life is much more fun to live.

Maybe you have some extra toys
That you can give away.
For those who don't have very much,
It will really make their day.

If you can earn some money
By doing an extra chore,
Maybe your parents will help you
Buy food at the grocery store.

As soon as your size changes,
The old clothes you can't wear
Can be given to other kids….
If clean and in good repair.

God loves your cheerful giving
To others you're among.
A habit of caring and sharing
Starts best when you are young.

"Serve one another in love."
Galatians 5:13

Kid Power

Children have power.
Honest, it's true.
Not the Super Hero Stuff...
Just the real you!

Using kind words
Can save the day,
When others fight
Instead of play.

Having good manners
Wherever you go,
Can cheer up some people
You don't even know.

Don't rush to be first.
Show patience in line.
If you can stay calm,
Then all will be fine.

Try making a card
When someone is sick.
It could help the person
To feel better quick.

Have faith in God's power
So you'll find a way
Of being a blessing
For someone today!

"Be kind to everyone."
2 Timothy 2:24

Instinct

Did you ever wonder how
A bird can build a nest?
They never go to nest school
Or need to take a test.

The answer is it's "instinct".
That's not a smell that stinks,
But a wonderful creation
Of ways an animal thinks.

Reptiles, amphibians, fish,
Birds, insects and such,
Know exactly what to do
Thanks to God's creative touch.

God made the sky above.
He made the land and sea.
God made the giant whale
And the tiny little bee.

God, thanks for all the animals
And this beautiful world we share.
May I be very careful
To treat each one with care.

"God made the world and everything in it."
Acts 17:24

Hooray for Glasses

Without my glasses on,
Things are blurry as can be.
I can't begin to read a book.
Even people look strange to me!

But when I put them on my face
So quickly I can see...
The beautiful world wherever I look;
Every flower. bird, and tree.

Thank you God for beauty.
Thanks for glasses to see.
Thank you for my blessings.
Thank you for making me.

"I love you, O Lord."

Psalm 18:1

Cheating is Not Smart

I really don't need to study,
Because I've got a buddy
That sits in the very next row.

Our desks are so near.
I can see quite clear
Any answers I really don't know.

But the test day came,
And oh what a shame,
I really was out of luck.

The rows had been changed,
The room rearranged,
And I knew that I was stuck!

God gave me a brain
With so much to gain,
Much more than just to get by.

And deep in my heart,
I'd like to be smart.
Maybe I'll give studying a try.

"Stop doing wrong and do good."
Psalm 34:14

Picking Teams

The class is picking teams again.
I wish I was home with the flu!
I know that I'll be chosen last.
That's what they always do.

I really try my very best,
Yet that is never enough.
When it comes to playing sports,
I just don't have the right stuff!

Someday I might get better.
I'll practice, wait, and see.
But in the meantime, I need a way
To be grateful just being me.

"God is with you wherever you go."

Joshua 1:9

Being a Good Sport

Always be a good sport...
Much easier said than done,
I'm only glad to do that
If my team has actually won!

When I've tried so very hard,
It's really super tough
To know that even doing my best
Just wasn't good enough.

Maybe I'll remember
When I don't act so nice,
That being a sore loser
Will only hurt me twice.

Because when I get grumpy
And show a nasty frown,
I only find I'm feeling worse
While bringing my team down.

Please God I need some help
On tough days when we lose.
I know I'd be a better sport
If I could walk in their shoes.

"Give thanks in all circumstances."
1 Thessalonians 5:18

The Bully

Nobody likes a bully,
So why should you even try?
Yet everyone is God's child,
And that's the reason why.

Here is how it happens
Inside a bully's heart.
A little like a see-saw,
Being "up" is the best part.

But in order to be up,
Someone else needs to be down.
And so for a quick moment,
A bully enjoys your frown.

Getting pushed or feelings hurt
Is certainly not any fun.
But if you give in to doing it too,
Then the bully has actually won.

So pray for God to give you
The courage to be kind.
Who knows? It might just be you
That changes the bully's mind!

"You are kind and forgiving, O Lord."

Psalm 86:5

A True Friend

"You have to do it my way,
Or I'm not going to be your friend."
"Again?" I said inside myself.
My patience was at an end!

I heard a voice that answered.
It sounded loud and clear.
Then I realized it was me
I was hearing in my ear!

"I'm sorry. I won't do it.
I really wish you'd stay.
But if you were my true friend
You wouldn't act this way."

Dear God, I hope that person
Will make a change someday.
I still want to be their friend.
It just can't be today.

"God will help you."
1 Chronicles 12:18

Hurting a Friend

When something breaks,
A tool it takes
To put it back together.

But what tool do you use
When a friend you might loose?
How do you make it better?

The tool that you try
Is the one you can't buy.
Say, "I'm sorry" right from your heart.

Then be sure to show
Kinder things that you know,
And you'll be off to a brand new start.

Just stick to the plan.
Do all that you can
To show your words were true.

And pray from your heart
To keep that new start.
For God wants joy for you!

"Forgive each other."
Colossians 3:13

Making Mistakes

My pencil made a mistake.
It certainly wasn't me.
I am always very careful
To do things perfectly.

I don't like to feel dumb
Or have others laugh at me.
It really hurts my feelings.
Sometimes my tears they see.

Why do some kids act so mean?
I really am confused.
Don't they understand how
I feel I'm being used?

Everyone makes mistakes.
My teacher said it's true.
Help me God to find a friend
Who understands that too.

"I will be glad and rejoice in your love."
Psalm 31:7

Computers

It isn't very easy
Being a child these days.
Children seem much smarter
In so many ways.

You're amazing with computers
And all technology.
But so much information
Needs a boundary.

So don't be sad and grumpy
When grown-ups make some rules.
They only want to help you
With all the learning tools.

Your childhood is so special.
There's really lots to do.
Of course God and your family
Want the best for you.

"Teach me your way, O Lord."
Psalm 86:11

Starting to Pray

How do I do it?
What should I say?
What words should I use
If I'm going to pray?

Do you think God can hear me?
Should I shout when I pray?
I know He lives in Heaven,
But that's really far away!

And since God is awake
Through both the night and day,
Maybe He's too tired
To hear me anyway.

Well that's enough to think about.
I'm not going to delay.
Okay God...ready or not,
I'm praying to you today.

"The Lord hears when I pray to him."
Psalm 4:3

Good Choices

God my Father
This I pray.
Help me use
My brain today.

May I own
The words I say.
Keep them kind
In every way.

Let my choices
When I play,
Cause my friends
To want to stay.

Keep me strong
When others may
Try their best
To make me stray.

I love you God!
I'll choose your way
Each time I use
My brain today.

"Hear the word of God and obey it."
Luke 11:28

Thankful Start

A thankful heart
Is a great place to start
When you begin your day.

Thank God for feet
And the people you'll meet
Passing by your way.

Thank God for arms
That have healing charms
From hugs you'll give today.

Thank God for faces
And all the great places
To give your smile away.

Thank God for love.
He's the Father above
Who listens when you pray.

Thank God for all.
No blessing is too small.
Be glad for a brand new day!

"Pray always and be thankful."
Colossians 4:2

Hearing God's Voice

There's an ear inside your heart.
Honest it is true.
Hide the letters h and t
Then you will see it too.

I think this might remind you
To listen with your heart,
For that's where God is talking
When you do the quiet part.

God waits for you to hear Him
So He can share with you,
To tell your heart and help your brain
Think what is best to do.

God's voice is more a feeling
Than talk like people make.
God's also a great listener
When time for prayer you take!

"Be still, and know that I am God!"

Psalm 46:10

Prayer Answers

Thank you God.
I know you are there.
Thank you God.
I'm glad that you care.

When I pray,
You hear every word.
Then answer best
To what you've heard.

Don't agree
With all that I say?
May I trust
Your choice anyway!

And answers
I want very quick,
Might not come
The speed you pick.

You love me
And I always know,
Your way is
The best to go.

"God gives us what we need."
Philippians 4:19

New Baby

I'm getting a sister
Or maybe a brother,
So I'll have to share
My father and mother.

They've got lots of love.
I don't need to worry.
As for sharing my stuff,
I'm not in a hurry!

And what if the baby
Cries all through the night?
Missing peaceful dreams
Would not be alright.

Well, enough of those thoughts
Dear God, help me be
The baby's best friend
In our whole family!

"Do what is right and good."
Deuteronomy 6:18

My Body

What's the big deal about my weight?
There's more to me than just what I ate!
Our bodies are built by God's design
And the many shapes are all just fine.

It's important to be glad for the body you've got.
Don't listen to others who think you should not.
Take care of it always, for goodness sake.
Eat healthy food so your tummy won't ache.

Exercise often and always get rest.
That will help you feel your best.
Skipping meals won't do the trick.
Then you'll just be skinny and sick.

Created by God who doesn't make mistakes,
He loves you and wants you free of heartaches.
Please don't believe the teasing and lies.
Pray for the strength to stop their tries.

Protect the body that was given to you.
Care for it always, and be proud of it too.
You were beautifully made by God above.
Treat your body with respect and yourself with love.

"By the grace of God I am what I am."
1 Corinthians 15:10

Feeling Sick

Today I have a fever
And my tummy has an ache.
I have to take some medicine
I don't really want to take.

What if I don't get better?
Next a doctor I will see.
If I need to get a shot
That's NOT okay with me!

I wish that I could go outside
And just play with a friend.
Oh, my body really hurts!
I know I can't pretend.

Please help me to be patient, God.
I know I need to rest.
Thanks for being with me
As I try to feel my best.

"Those who wait on the Lord
will renew their strength."
Isaiah 40:31

Moving Away

My parents said we're moving.
I can't believe it's true.
They didn't even ask me
What I wanted to do.

I guess they knew my answer.
No way! No chance! No how!
I like my school and all my friends.
Life's really fine right now.

Okay, I'm not the only kid
Who's ever had to move.
I guess I need to say a prayer
That God will make it smooth.

If someone tries to chase me
Or use mean words to tease,
Please promise to be near me
And help my fears to ease.

I know I've been a good friend
When other kids are new.
I pray that God will help me
Find others who will too.

"Honor your father and your mother."

Exodus 20:12

Divorce Hurts

I felt just like a doughnut
With a great big hole inside.
My parents said they're getting divorced.
My anger was hard to hide.

I went to school like always
And tried to act the same.
My parents said it wasn't my fault,
But I really felt the shame.

I'm glad my teacher noticed
The sadness showing through.
I was so surprised to find out
Her parents had been divorced too!

There's nothing I can do now.
I can't fix my family.
Of course I'll pray and love them.
And I also need prayers for me!

"Pray to God, and he will hear you."

Job 22:27

Pet Passing

I cried and cried
The day my pet died.
I was sure I'd never get better.

Each thought I had
Made me even more sad,
And my face just kept getting wetter.

Then through my pain,
An idea hit my brain
To write my pet a letter.

I asked God to listen
To the things I had written
About our time together.

And when I was through,
I definitely knew
I was already feeling much better.

"My eye pours out tears to God."
Job 16:20

Promoted to Heaven

Especially when someone dies,
Life seems to be unclear.
God understands your sadness
And every little tear.

Just like being promoted...
At school from grade to grade,
There's a final promotion to Heaven.
It's a promise God has made.

God's home has lots of rooms.
It's a beautiful place to be.
No sickness and no sadness...
Just joy and harmony.

All human bodies die, we know.
Some are old and some are not.
But then each spirit can live with God.
His word, for sure, we've got!

"I trust in God's word."
Psalm 119:42

God Doesn't Snore

I'm really very sure
That God doesn't snore.
That's because He doesn't sleep!

God's awake all night
While I close my eyes tight,
With dreams so sweet and deep.

But sometimes I'm mad
When a nightmare I've had.
I'm so scared, I can't make a peep.

Then God is still near
To help with my fear
So I can go back to sleep.

"In God I trust; I will not be afraid."
Psalm 56:4

Printed in the United States
By Bookmasters